When Kings Rule and Priest Sacrifice

RUTHANN JOHNSON

Copyright © 2024 Ruthann Johnson

All Rights Reserved. No part of this book may be used or reproduced by any means, graphic, electronic, or mechanical, including photocopying, recording, taping, or by any information storage retrieval system without the written permission of the publisher except in the case of brief quotations embodied in critical articles and reviews.

Unless otherwise identified, Scripture quotations are taken from the King James Version (KJV).

Scripture quotations marked AMP are taken from the Amplified Bible copyright © 2015 by The Lockman Foundation, La Habra, CA 90631. All rights reserved.

Scripture quotations marked AMPC are taken from the Amplified Bible, Classic Edition. Copyright © 1954, 1958, 1962, 1964, 1965, 1987 by The Lockman Foundation. All rights reserved.

Scripture quotations marked EASY are taken from the EasyEnglish Bible Copyright © MissionAssist 2019 - Charitable Incorporated Organisation 1162807. Used by permission. All rights reserved.

Scripture quotations marked ERV are taken from the Easy-to-Read Version. Copyright © 2006 by Bible League International.

Scripture quotations marked ESV are taken from The Holy Bible, English Standard Version® (ESV®), copyright © 2001 by Crossway, a publishing ministry of Good News Publishers.

Scripture quotations marked (MSG) are from THE MESSAGE. The Bible in Contemporary Language copyright © 1993, 2002, 2018 by Eugene H. Peterson. All rights reserved. Used by permission of NavPress. Represented by Tyndale House Publishers.

Scripture quotations marked NLT are taken from the Holy Bible, New Living Translation, copyright © 1996, 2004, 2015 by Tyndale House Foundation. Used by permission of Tyndale House Publishers, Inc., Carol Stream, Illinois 60188. All rights reserved.

Scripture quotations marked PHILLIPS are taken from the New Testament in Modern English by J.B Phillips copyright © 1960, 1972 J. B. Phillips. Administered by The Archbishops' Council of the Church of England. Used by Permission.

Scripture quotations marked TPT are from The Passion Translation®. Copyright © 2017, 2018, 2020 by Passion & Fire Ministries, Inc. Used by permission. All rights reserved.

When Kings Rule and Priest Sacrifice

TABLE OF CONTENT

Acknowledgment vi

Prelude vii

The Attitude of the Priest 1

The Builder's Anointing................................. 7

The Key to Greatness 19

What motivates you? 29

ACKNOWLEDGMENT

To my family, friends, those I have the privilege of serving alongside in my local church, those I've served with over the years, and to my leaders, thank you.

God, in His sovereignty, was gracious enough to allow me to learn by will or by force the lessons this book contains; for that and for you, I am grateful.

PRELUDE

I didn't understand what I was doing; I thought I was doing them a favor. I didn't realize that I was only hurting myself when I walked out of that meeting, telling them that when they were ready for my abilities, they should let me know.

I was in my early 20s serving in the Youth Ministry, and when I got offended, I eventually resigned from my position. At the time, I felt justified, after all, I was mishandled, and they were ungrateful and unsupportive. I couldn't see that it was a test, and I had failed miserably, so much so that I would need spiritual remedial classes. In my books; 'The Art of Transition' and 'Pride ain't Prejudice,' I mentioned the challenges I experienced in the marriage, but deep in my heart, I knew it was as a result of how I handled that test a few seasons before.

As gifted as I am, I wasn't allowed to use them in the marriage, I was relegated to just being a maid.

As bitter as I was toward my ex-husband, I knew God allowed it, and the one thing I kept saying was, "God, the heart of the king is in your hand; you can turn it however you please, but you're allowing him to treat me like this."

That season taught me that serving is a privilege.

It is my prayer that as you read this book, you will be infused with Holy Fear and reverence for the work God has called you to within the body of Christ, not just as a king but also as a priest.

This book is designed to remind us of the principles that govern this ancient *virtue* called 'Serving' and to inspire us to do it with the highest level of excellence as unto the Lord.

.

THE ATTITUDE OF THE PRIEST

Priest. . .they were devoted to the temple, they served, they sacrificed.

Our kingly duties don't replace our priestly duties; we have to learn how to do both, which means serving our region externally and still serving our house locally.

As believers, we have been adopted into God's royal family, and we have been given divine authority to function as kingdom ambassadors on the earth. With this authority comes responsibilities and protocols that govern how we conduct ourselves.

Revelation 5:10 NLT
"And you have caused them to become a Kingdom of priests for our God. And they will reign on the earth."

According to Revelation 5:10, we are not just royal ambassadors; we're also priests, and that is the foundation or premise of this book. As we govern the jurisdictions God has entrusted us, we should remember that our kingly duties don't replace our priestly duties. We have to learn how to do both, in that we serve not just our careers or businesses but also our place of worship locally.

THE PRIEST

As 'priests'[1] we officiate, which means that there are certain religious services or duties that we're expected to perform, one of which involves making sacrifices, but it's not the sacrifice of bulls as they did in the Old Testament, nor is it the physical sacrifice on the cross which Christ has already done. It's the kind of sacrifice that requires our unwavering commitment to advancing God's agenda in the earthly realm. But how do we do this? It starts in the local church, so Paul encourages us not to forsake the assembling of ourselves together.

Hebrews 10:25 PHILLIPS
"And let us not hold aloof from our church meetings, as some do. Let us do all we can to help one another's faith, and this the more earnestly as we see the final day drawing ever nearer."

---

[1] H3548 - kōhēn - Strong's Hebrew Lexicon (kjv). Retrieved from https://www.blueletterbible.org/lexicon/h3548/kjv/wlc/0-1/

Romans 12:1 EASY

"My Christian friends, God has been very kind to us. Because of that, I really want you to serve God with your whole life. Offer your bodies to him like a sacrifice that continues to live. Serve him with everything that you have, and that will please him. That is the true way to worship God."

But why is it so important for us to come together? What do we do when we come together? The reality is that God has not changed His mind about salvation, and in order for us to share this great gospel, we need men and women who are committed to being agents of change. Paul said,

Romans 10:13-15 TPT

"And it's true: "Everyone who calls on the Lord's name will experience new life." But how can people call on him for help if they've not yet believed? And how can they believe in one they've not yet heard of? And how can they hear the message of life if there is no one there to proclaim it? And how can the message be proclaimed if messengers have yet to be sent? That's why the Scriptures say: How welcome is the arrival of those proclaiming the joyful news of peace and of good things to come!"

The preacher, in any capacity, whether it's the person teaching a sermon or the one encouraging someone in the store, has to be cultivated somewhere. We have to willingly submit ourselves to the process of maturing into the image of Christ.

This process involves people because we're fitly joined together, supplying what each other needs. This is why, today we sacrifice by honoring our commitment to serve the body of Christ in our local assembly. As we serve, our character is developed and our spiritual credibility report is being created so that God can trust us to rule and represent Him well in our different spheres of influence.

We serve with the understanding that, like Samuel, we're being groomed, and our function has a dual impact. We do it with a reverential fear because it's a sacred privilege. We've read chapter after chapter of kings who forsook God and failed miserably, so we should not expect to effectively produce any lasting impact that brings glory to God outside of our priesthood.

Priest sacrifice, our lives are the sacrifice, our opinions are the sacrifice, our desires are the sacrifice, our way; that's what we sacrifice. The more we serve, the more opportunities we have to grow.

What's the attitude of the priest?

He has decided to become a "willing" sacrifice. His heart's song is, "Yes, Lord."

THE BUILDER'S ANOINTING

We don't realize how significant our part is, so we become casual.

Nehemiah 6:3 AMP
"So I sent messengers to them, saying, "I am doing a great work and cannot come down. Why should the work stop while I leave to come down to [meet with] you?""

Casual, so we don't expect demonic opposition, but as we serve, let us watch and pray because priest also intercedes.

Organigram

In order for us to effectively supply what the body needs, we have to first identify the different parts of the body and how each part functions. In businesses, they create 'organizational charts' to provide a breakdown of the responsibilities or roles of each employee within that organization.

The ancient principle of identifying and assigning responsibilities started at the beginning of time when God created the heavens and the earth along with everything in it, then Adam and gave him dominion. His first order of business was to name the animals. Within each name was the nature of the animal, its capabilities, responsibilities, and limitations.

This is so important because it helps us to avoid unnecessary confusion, unrealistic expectations, and incompetence. It doesn't matter how persistent a snail is; it will never be able to move as fast as a gazelle, so it would be unrealistic to expect it to move as fast. The snail could also be seen as incompetent if required to move as fast as a gazelle when that speed is simply beyond its capacity.

Unfortunately, we don't always know how to function effectively within the body because we're still trying to identify who we are. This is why we must exercise the fruit of the Spirit by being patient with each other, knowing that little by little, as we are serving, we discover our capabilities and our limitations.

In the book of Exodus chapter 3, God gave Moses specific instructions about not just the dimensions of the Tabernacle but who had the capabilities to build different aspects of it.

Exodus 31:1-6 NLT

"Then the Lord said to Moses, "Look, I have specifically chosen Bezalel son of Uri, grandson of Hur, of the tribe of Judah. I have filled him with the Spirit of God, giving him great wisdom, ability, and expertise in all kinds of crafts. He is a master craftsman, expert in working with gold, silver, and bronze. He is skilled in engraving and mounting gemstones and in carving wood. He is a master at every craft! "And I have personally appointed Oholiab son of Ahisamach, of the tribe of Dan, to be his assistant. Moreover, I have given special skill to all the gifted craftsmen so they can make all the things I have commanded you to make:"

In some instances, God does instruct us directly or through the leaders He's set over us to do specific tasks or to serve in specific areas based on what He's deposited in us, whether we're aware of it or not. For Bezalel, being a master craftsman meant that he was aware of his innate ability and would've cultivated a certain level of mastery over time, so when Moses gave him the assignment, his responsibilities with the overall completion of the Tabernacle were clear.

A builder knows that the vision dictates the workforce, so every church's organizational structure won't be the same because their assignment or vision is not the same. So, in Exodus, after Moses got the instructions from God, he knew exactly what the vision was and the criteria the people needed to meet to effectively aid in accomplishing that vision. Everyone was given the same assignment, or the measure was distributed based on each person's capacity. This is important so that we don't compare ourselves or different ministries to each other and try to take on responsibilities beyond our capacity. That's what causes unnecessary frustration or confusion.

Unlike Moses, Solomon didn't get the name of the craftsman from God, so he had to rely on the people to be honest about their capabilities in order to employ the right workforce to build the temple. His father had already selected craftsmen, but he recognized that they were not capable of doing all the work by themselves. In 2 Chronicles, we see where he did a census, which would've helped him evaluate the people to know what area they could work in.

2 Chronicles 2:1-3,7,11,13-14,17 NLT

"Solomon decided to build a Temple to honor the name of the Lord, and also a royal palace for himself. He enlisted a force of 70,000 laborers, 80,000 men to quarry stone in the hill country, and 3,600 foremen. Solomon also sent this message to King Hiram at Tyre: Send me cedar logs as you did for my father, David, when he was building his palace. "So send me a master craftsman who can work with gold, silver, bronze, and iron, as well as with purple, scarlet, and blue cloth. He must be a skilled engraver who can work with the craftsmen of Judah and Jerusalem who were selected by my father, David. King Hiram sent this letter of reply to Solomon: "I am sending you a master craftsman named Huram-abi, who is extremely talented. He is skillful at making things from gold, silver, bronze, and iron, and he also works with stone and wood. He can work with purple, blue, and scarlet cloth and fine linen. He is also an engraver and can follow any design given to him. "

If Huram-abi could only work with gold and bronze, not silver and iron, or if he was just a craftsman and not necessarily a specialist, he would not have been the best fit for that assignment because Solomon already had craftsmen. If he, out of pride or sincerity, accepted the assignment without the right skill set, it would've impeded the work and become a burden to himself.

As we serve in the body, we will be given assignments that are designed to help us expand our capacity, while others will simply be outside of our parameters, which means that for us to be effective, we have to be honest and transparent with our leaders and those we serve with.

THE BUILDER'S WARFARE

The Bible says that Solomon **"decided to build"** the temple. When we agree to serve in our local church, we are **'deciding to build'** the house of the Lord and to advance His kingdom. We have to be resolute in this decision because even with our best efforts to put people in the right positions and to foster healthy communication, we will have opposition.

At times there'll be inadequate resources to do the work, and we'll also have misunderstandings and conflicts, but this is all a part of our character development and should never be used as an excuse to stop serving.

Luke 9:62 EASY

"Jesus replied, 'A man that ploughs a field must continue to look straight in front of him. If he looks behind him, he cannot plough well. People that look back behind them cannot work well for the kingdom of God.'"

As we serve, we'll experience discouragement or disappointment in not only our teammates but also ourselves when we don't accomplish what our hearts desire. When these things happen, we should see them as God shining a light on areas that need to be developed, whether personally or organizationally. It could be seen as a 'Breach Inspector' because it's not just an opportunity for us to identify the fruit of the spirit we're lacking, but it also helps us address wounds in our souls that we haven't addressed or don't even realize exist.

Some assignments will be difficult, and so will the people we may have to serve with. We will be tempted to quit, but don't quit. See it as the refiner's fire, see it as being molded on the potter's wheel. Don't lose sight of the truth that as we serve, we're making an impact that goes beyond the four walls of our local house, one that will change lives and cause people to come to know God.

We serve as unto the Lord; that's why we . . .
- apologize even if we don't want to,
- speak the truth in love,
- make allowance for each other's faults,
- take the lower seat and give up our rights for the sake of peace,
- honor our commitments,
- don't murmur or complain,
- promote unity and encourage each other.

Tempted to waver, but don't become weary in well-doing.

Sometimes, our frustration is misdirected because our perception is off, meaning that the problem isn't always a lack of resources. The Bible tells us that Solomon did a census, which implies that before he sent the request to the king, he did a thorough assessment of the resources that were already at his disposal. Therefore, it's important that we periodically evaluate not just our teams but the systems. People outgrow positions, and systems become obsolete, so to remain effective, we must implement structures that will facilitate people's smooth transition from one area to the next, as well as workflows that will alert us of any potential system malfunctions.

In Solomon's case, he had 3,600 foremen who were responsible for overseeing the workers. In organizations, we call it the Human Resources Department, but within the local church, it's simply an accountability system that requires leaders to provide updates on the welfare of the people and the operations within their department.

Builders attract resources

But what happens when we've done our assessments and utilized the resources we have but still struggle to be effective? What happens when a person feels like they're being stretched beyond their capacity? In 2 Chronicles 3, King Hiram sent King Solomon a master craftsman who could do more than he had requested.

2 Chronicles 2:14 NLT

"His mother is from the tribe of Dan in Israel, and his father is from Tyre. He is skillful at making things from gold, silver, bronze, and iron, and he also works with stone and wood. He can work with purple, blue, and scarlet cloth and fine linen. He is also an engraver and can follow any design given to him. He will work with your craftsmen and those appointed by my lord David, your father."

Ultimately, this is the Lord's house and His work, but sometimes, the enemy allows us to accept a false burden of feeling adequate when the work gets difficult or demanding. So, we have to learn to rest in God's grace and trust that He will send us the right tools or people to accomplish the vision of the house.

THE KEY TO GREATNESS

My mother always said, "There are gifts in you that you haven't discovered yet". Over the years I've realized that serving helped me discover them.

Mark 10:42-45 TPT

"Jesus gathered them all together and said to them, "Those recognized as rulers of the people and those who are in top leadership positions rule oppressively over their subjects, but this is not the example you are to follow. You are to lead by a different model. If you want to be the greatest, then live as one called to serve others. The path to promotion comes by having the heart of a bond-slave who serves everyone. For even the Son of Man did not come expecting to be served by everyone, but to serve everyone, and to give his life as the ransom price for the salvation of many.""

As believers, we lead by a different model, we are priests, we sacrifice, and we serve. In serving and adding value to people's lives, that's how we become great. It's not the kind of greatness the world promotes even in 'overnight success' it is like the sacrifice Christ made in serving himself for us to receive salvation by faith. He left an indelible mark, and His greatness transcended dimensions. There is no currency adequate enough to quantify His greatness; it's beyond superficial, and no analytics could accurately report His impact. We're still benefiting from His "service" to humanity. So my question is, what kind of greatness are we in pursuit of? Is it to be seen by men?

If we want to be *great* in spiritual ranking that gives us authority over demonic powers, we can't forsake our priesthood. We shouldn't neglect our spiritual responsibility of living a sacrificial life before God; that includes serving. Serve in intercession, serve in the giving of our time and efforts to add value to someone else's life, and serve in building our local church so that the gospel can continue to reach the lost and dying.

God's refinery

If we want to exemplify *great* character, serve. It's the refiner's fire that deals with the impurities in our souls. In serving, the conflicts, the friction, and the tension are what highlight our character flaws and give us a safe space to work on them so that we don't attain great possessions or positions and later break under the weight of it. So that we don't fail where many mighty men have fallen. Serving is powerful, it keeps us humble.

It is our priesthood that makes us different from the kings of this world; it's our subjection to a life of complete devotion to God that sets us apart and empowers us to not just attain influence but maintain our integrity. We dare not aspire to rule in any jurisdiction, in any place where we have not erected an altar unto the Lord.

What does this mean? Solomon said

2 Chronicles 2:4-6 NLT
"I am about to build a Temple to honor the name of the Lord my God. It will be a place set apart to burn fragrant incense before him, to display the special sacrificial bread, and to sacrifice burnt offerings each morning and evening, on the Sabbaths, at new moon celebrations, and at the other appointed festivals of the Lord our God. He has commanded Israel to do these things forever. "This must be a magnificent Temple because our God is greater than all other gods. But who can really build him a worthy home? Not even the highest heavens can contain him! So who am I to consider building a Temple for him, except as a place to burn sacrifices to him?"

Before we rule, we need an altar. We need a place where we rend our hearts before the Lord; we need a place where our flesh dies; we need a place where we're submitted to authority, where we are compelled to walk in humility. It happens through serving; it's the way of the priest, it secures our seat. He has commanded us to do this forever: the higher we go, the more influence we attain, the more promotions we accomplish in our careers, and the more successful we become in our businesses, the more devoted we should be to this ancient virtue called 'serving.'

THE ENEMY OF GREATNESS

Proverbs 16:18-19 TPT
"Your boast becomes a prophecy of a future failure. The higher you lift yourself up in pride, the harder you'll fall in disgrace. It's better to be meek and lowly and live among the poor than to live high and mighty among the rich and famous."

Serving keeps us humble; it deals with the pride in us. It forces us to stay low, to remain humanly subjective, in that we don't allow the things we've attained to make us think that we no longer need God. When we serve and experience hostility or challenges, it prevents idolatry, so we don't worship our titles and positions.

THE REWARDS OF SERVING

- *<u>Serving has a sound, it makes a signal:</u>*

    - It activates refreshing

"Whoever brings blessing will be enriched, and one who waters will himself be watered." Proverbs 11:25 ESV

    - It's a privilege

"One day spent in your house, this beautiful place of worship, beats thousands spent on Greek island beaches. I'd rather scrub floors in the house of my God than be honored as a guest in the palace of sin." - Psalms 84:10 MSG

- It's a favor magnet

"One day Ruth the Moabite said to Naomi, "Let me go out into the harvest fields to pick up the stalks of grain left behind by anyone who is kind enough to let me do it." Naomi replied, "All right, my daughter, go ahead." So Ruth went out to gather grain behind the harvesters. And as it happened, she found herself working in a field that belonged to Boaz, the relative of her father-in-law, Elimelech. <u>While she was there, Boaz arrived</u> from Bethlehem and greeted the harvesters. "The Lord be with you!" he said. "The Lord bless you!" the harvesters replied. Then Boaz asked his foreman, "Who is that young woman over there? Who does she belong to?" And the foreman replied, "She is the young woman from Moab who came back with Naomi. She asked me this morning if she could gather grain behind the harvesters. <u>She has been hard at work ever since, except for a few minutes' rest in the shelter.</u>" Boaz went over and said to Ruth, "Listen, my daughter. Stay right here with us when you gather grain; don't go to any other fields. Stay right behind the young women working in my field. See which part of the field they are harvesting, and then follow them. I have warned the young men not to treat you roughly. And when you are thirsty, help yourself to the water they have drawn from the well." Ruth fell at his feet and thanked him warmly. <u>"What have I done to deserve such kindness?"</u> she asked. <u>"I am only a foreigner."</u> "Yes, I know," Boaz replied. "But I also know about everything you have done for your mother-in-law since the death of your husband. I have heard how you left your father and mother and your own land to live here among complete strangers. **May the Lord, the God of Israel, under whose wings you have come to take refuge, reward you fully for what you have done.'"** - Ruth 2:2-12 NLT

Serving is the key to mastery

As you serve, you're becoming better and better; your gifts are developed, and you also build consistency.

It's a Weapon, it's a shield

Within about three months of my relocation after the marital separation, I started serving in the media department at my local church. I didn't realize that as I kept serving, the Word of God was penetrating my soul. It became a weapon against depression and suicide because it consumed most of my time. Each time I had to re-watch a sermon to review camera shots, the Word was getting in.

Whenever I had to show up to run the livestream during 5:00 AM Prayers, the Word kept washing me, refreshing my soul, and healing places I didn't know how to verbalize.

Serving is like an ecosystem, where everything you need is in one place. The Bible calls it, being fitly joined together, supplying what each other needs.

Do you need . . .

- <u>Community, friendship, or accountability</u>

He puts the solitary in families.

Serving disarms the enemy and prevents him from convincing a believer that no one cares about them. It provides a safety net for those who are vulnerable and allows them to be covered until they recover. It gives them a sense of belonging and assurance that they're not in this fight all by themselves.

- To discover your purpose
  - Uncertain of your true identity? Start serving.
  - Don't know what you're good at? Serve.
  - Feel like you don't have any talents? Serve.

There are gifts in us that we haven't discovered yet, and sometimes, God allows those we labor with to help us identify them.

WHAT MOTIVATES YOU?

Jesus never had a marketing team - He just served Himself to the world.

Serving is a privilege given to us. When we are asked to serve, we should see it as if we have been awarded a scholarship that will further our spiritual development.

Sometimes, if we're not careful, we could find ourselves treating the house of God like an internship[2] where we gain experience relating to our careers or interests. The place we practice for the secular stage or solicit clients, abusing our authority or access to the people God has entrusted to us. There's a very thin line between favor and exploitation.

The lines get crossed when we lose the fear of God for His work and His people. When the lines are crossed, we find ourselves taking advantage of the people as they come to bring their offerings to God the way Eli's sons did. It's easy to deceive ourselves into thinking we're not like them because theirs was sexual and ours isn't but let's define exploitation:

Definition:
According to the dictionary, to exploit means to:
- make full use of and derive benefit from (a resource).

---

[2] https://careers.umbc.edu/employers/internships/what-is-an-internship/

- use (a situation or person) in an unfair or selfish way.
- benefit unfairly from the work of (someone), typically by overworking or underpaying them.

On the other hand, when someone is favored, it means that they've been the recipient of an overgenerous preferential treatment without compulsion or manipulation.

Influence is a byproduct of serving, especially when we serve well. However, we must never abuse it. The priests had access to God's inner chambers; they were privy to confidential information and they had to walk in integrity.

1 Samuel 12:3-4 AMP

"Here I am; testify against me before the Lord and [Saul] His anointed [if I have done someone wrong]. Whose ox have I taken, or whose donkey have I taken, or whom have I exploited? Whom have I oppressed or from whose hand have I taken a bribe to blind my eyes [to the truth]? [Tell me and] I will restore it to you." They said, "You have not exploited us or oppressed us or taken anything at all from a man's hand."

Being integral isn't just for the leaders, it's for all of us, we're all priests under the new covenant. Are we willing to be the priests who stand before the people blameless?

WHAT IS REQUIRED OF US

As priests, we are held to a higher standard; we govern our lives according to the moral codes written in the word of God. Our priesthood doesn't begin in service when we're on duty; it's a lifestyle of honoring God so that our character will bear scrutiny no matter the department or area of the body we serve.

Leviticus 21:6 EASY
"Priests must be holy to serve me. They must not bring shame to the name of their God. They are the people who offer gifts to the Lord. They bring food to their God. So they must be holy people."

If someone were to take a look under our internal hood to see what's driving us, what would they find? Why do we serve the way we do? Why are we so passionate? Is it love, or are we motivated by strife and jealousy?

- <u>Are you trying to get attention?</u>

"A gift gets attention; it buys the attention of eminent people." - Proverbs 18:16 MSG

- <u>Are you trying to get your foot in the door?</u>

"Gifts can open many doors and help you meet important people." - Proverbs 18:16 ERV

- <u>Are you trying to meet important people?</u>

"Would you like to meet a very important person? Take a generous gift. It will do wonders to gain entrance into his presence." - Proverbs 18:16 TPT

Our motives matter and so do our attitudes. . .

•

In the book of 1 Peter, the Bible charges us to serve as Holy priests. It said,

1 Peter 2:5 TPT
"Come and be his "living stones" who are continually being assembled into a sanctuary for God. For now you serve as holy priests, offering up spiritual sacrifices that he readily accepts through Jesus Christ."

PRIESTLY PROTOCOLS

Exodus 31:11 EASY
"the special oil to show that things belong to me, and the sweet incense for the Holy Place. The workers must make all these things in the way that I have commanded you.'"

When it comes to serving, we don't get to do whatever we want to do. There are protocols that govern a local assembly, and when we commit to serving in that ministry, we have to abide by the standards of operation that they've implemented, whether we think we have a better idea or not.

We don't submit to abuse or immorality, nor do we comply with anything that goes against the written word of God. We also don't manipulate the Word of God to appease our flesh and promote rebellion.

THE PRIESTLY OATH

My prayer is that this book would've ignited a reverential fear for serving in the house of the Lord. I leave us with this charge from the Apostle Peter:

"So abandon every form of evil, deceit, hypocrisy, feelings of jealousy and slander." - 1 Peter 2:1 TPT

"SO BE done with every trace of wickedness (depravity, malignity) and all deceit and insincerity (pretense, hypocrisy) and grudges (envy, jealousy) and slander and evil speaking of every kind." - 1 Peter 2:1 AMPC

As servants of God, serving in any capacity.

From the Apostle Paul,

"Servants (slaves), be obedient to those who are your physical masters, having respect for them and eager concern to please them, in singleness of motive and with all your heart, as [service] to Christ [Himself]– Not in the way of eye-service [as if they were watching you] and only to please men, but as servants (slaves) of Christ, doing the will of God heartily and with your whole soul;" - Ephesians 6:5-6 AMPC

As David said,

"Serve the Lord with reverent awe and worshipful fear; rejoice and be in high spirits with trembling [lest you displease Him]." - Psalm 2:11 AMPC

ABOUT THE AUTHOR

Ruthann Johnson is a gem whose life is committed to advancing the kingdom of God. She's a strategist who is constantly seeking ways of becoming more effective.

OTHER BOOKS

Ruthann has also written:

- The Heart of Serving like a Priest - the serving workbook designed to provide practical tips to help the believer identify the areas they could serve in.
- The Art of Transition - learn to experience maximum productivity in what seems to be the most difficult seasons of your life.
- Pride ain't Prejudice - learn about overcoming childhood trauma and being a standard bearer who lives a life of sexual purity to the glory of God.

LOVED READING THIS BOOK?

GIVE IT AWAY!

If reading this book has impacted your life and you would like to order more copies for those in your sphere of influence (perhaps your church, small group, company, friends, or family), please don't hesitate to get in touch with us to get a discount on a bulk order at:
ruthann.c@icloud.com.

OTHER PROJECTS

Ruthann has also served the body in other capacities:

- Open Pockets - A Finance Podcast where she shares biblical principles to empower listeners to become better stewards of their finances. It's aired Thursdays [bi-weekly] on several podcast platforms.
- CHRISTIANE - A clothing line that specializes in clothing alterations infused with scriptures from the Word of God, with some designs being hand-stitched beaded work.

For more information on any of these products or services, feel free to view her link-tree page @ruthannchristiane for the latest updates.

www.ingramcontent.com/pod-product-compliance
Lightning Source LLC
Chambersburg PA
CBHW070543080426
42453CB00029B/1023